Love Most Of You Too

Dustin Brookshire

Harbor Editions
Small Harbor Publishing

Cover art *Fiction Flats* by C.R. Resetarits
first published by *CURA: A Literary Magazine of Action*
Cover design by Taylor Blevins
Book layout by Allison Blevins and Hannah Martin

LOVE MOST OF YOU TOO
DUSTIN BROOKSHIRE
ISBN 978-1-7359090-3-5
Harbor Editions,
an imprint of Small Harbor Publishing

*To my primary and secondary English/Literature teachers—
thank you for making me feel seen, safe, and encouraging me to
write: Reba Carpenter, 3rd & 5th grades; Vicki Dillard, 7th
grade; Angela Harris, 10th grade; and Darlene Callan, 12th
grade. And, to my high school journalism teacher, Renee Lloyd,
9th-12th grades.*

*To the Literature teacher who didn't encourage me, made me feel
small, and told me to stop writing poems—
Nancy Ratcliffe (11th grade), this is also for you.*

CONTENTS

Love Most Of You Too

WANTING TO COME OUT

Thirteen, in the bathroom, with my brother's razor,
door locked, drawers pulled out to barricade,
I sat not wanting to bring razor across flesh,
not wanting to live a life explaining a scar
even though, now, I realize that's all we do,
explain our scars to one another
and hope for understanding.

I sat slouched on the floor, back to wall,
staring at my feet to avoid my reflection.
I sat with razor in hand.
I can't be more honest when I say
I didn't want to slit my wrists,
only needed to hear,
We love you.

Fists pummeled the door.
My brother yelled,
What the hell are you thinking?

We never spoke of that night again.

BAD FRUIT

inspired by Denise Duhamel's "Apple"

You're a bad apple, says my aunt.
She's thankful I fell from a different tree.
I won't argue. Three of her four never
graduated high school. All had shotgun weddings,
and I write letters to one in a Florida prison.
He was on the news—seemed like every channel,
but I'm the apple whose seeds won't bear fruit,
which makes me bad as gay can be.
How does she speak of her son? The robbery.
An unarmed man shot in the back of the head.
How does she explain the fruit she bore
when it is absolutely rotten to the core?

ON LINE DANCING NIGHT AT THE GAY BAR I THINK OF MY GRANDMA

Because she watched CMT
with the dedication
holy rollers attend church,
because I would sing Shania
but especially Reba,
and even though
I couldn't carry a tune
strapped to my back,
she smiled, waved, and cheered
from her couch,
because when I came out
my mother asked,
What would your grandmother think?

I knew: *She* would love me.

SIGNS

My mother dreams of dark running water.
She calls. It is the death dream.
I follow the speed limit.
I walk faster than normal through crosswalks.
I am even more careful when showering,
a fall now seems more probable.
When I was a child she told me
the secret of this dream—
someone would die
but she wouldn't know who.
The dream came when my grandmother
was admitted to the hospital,
when a family friend
was supposed to be winning
her battle with cancer. Once
it came and she couldn't think
of anyone sick, my father's favorite
employee was hit by a car.
I told you, she whispered.
I prayed to God—begged Him
not to pass this curse to me.
As a teenager I thought
the world one of coincidence—
that there aren't signs placed
to tell us what will come.
But, yesterday,
I was in a Knoxville bar
with Julie, trying to forget
my worries, when I looked up
and noticed we were sitting under
a poster of Dolly Parton.
This moment a sign.

THIS POEM WANTS TO BE CENSORED

This poem wants to cause a ruckus
like Janet Jackson's pierced nipple—
give the right wing more than a nipple ring
to sink their communion-taking mouths into.

This poem says bring the black permanent markers
to mark out its lines like school officials
in New Jersey blacked out the yearbook picture
of two male students kissing.

This poem says strike a match
to the page on which it is written:
you Hitler-wanna-be motherfucker.
This poem is ready to blaze.

This poem has no problem saying
fuck the Patriot Act. If you think
library records are telling,
then this poem wants to know
if reading Edward Hirsch's *How to Read a Poem*
classifies it as a terrorist.

This poem loves to be dirty and true—
to say getting rid of Bush was needed
because a bush only gets in the way.

Yes. This poem is begging to be censored.
This poem knows, unlike those who would censor,
censorship will only make the world want it more.

NIGHTMARE

I'm here! I'm here!
I scream in my dream,
the same one
I've had for weeks.
I'm at the doctor's office—
ten pounds lost
and a bloody cough.
The nurse calls my name.
I stand.
She continues to call.
Coming, I say.
But she continues to call.
Coming, I say walking toward her
as she continues to call
as she stares through me.
I scream, *I'm here! I'm here!*
She turns around,
closes the door in my face
while I cough and cough,
stare at the blood in my hand,
stare at the waiting room, empty
except for the coffin, so close
I can touch it when I wake.

MEMO

She tells me her soon-to-be ex-husband
is complaining to mutual friends about her wanting
half of everything—to sell the mountain home
and condo in Key West—to split it all evenly
like a baker halving a loaf of bread.
I don't pity him. He's fucking his secretary,
so man-mid-life-crisis-typical,
which only means a convertible is next.
I want to call him, tell him she deserves
more than half, and if I were her, I'd send
his mistress a memo: his balls in a Ziploc bag.
My friend insists he isn't worth the time,
swears the secretary will get what she deserves
the day she says, *I do*.

AUNT WITH A MISSION

Have you asked God to forgive your sin?
She asks with no love in her eyes.
His power can change you back again.

Battles over the *Bible*, with her, I can't win.
She prefers I live a lie.
Have you asked God to forgive your sin?

Adamant in her quest since I'm kin.
My being gay makes her cry,
His power can change you back again.

I see she wears her crucifix pin,
her cross to bear until she dies.
Have you asked God to forgive your sin?

Disgusted by my attraction to men
she tells me I must, I must try—
His power can change you back again.

Satan has him. Where did it begin?
words from mouth, to Heaven they fly,
Have you asked God to forgive your sin?
His power can change you back again.

TO TERI HATCHER WITH LOVE
for Geoff

I have it on good authority that Teri Hatcher
started an email to her *Desperate Housewives* costars
    with
Listen, you bitches.
My mouth left wide open after hearing this scoop.
Really, I exclaimed.
I saw a copy of the email, a friend verified.
Maybe you should send it to me, I coaxed.
I'm not losing my job, he or she replied.
This was the moment I started to like Teri Hatcher.
I came to peace with her character
on *Desperate Housewives*, who always annoyed me—
Watch-Me-Be-Cute-And-Trip-Over-Air Susan
or I'm-Desperate-To-Get-Mike-At-All-Costs-
    Season-1 Susan.
I often wished for Teri's character to be written off,
but then it happened—like an epiphany
at the end of a season. I suddenly loved Teri Hatcher.
I cheered for Susan,
even laughed when she tripped over nothing.
Yes, you want to know
the dirt behind the *Listen you bitches* email,
but the email is not the point of this poem.
The point is we're capable of doing a 180
when someone else has the balls
or brass ovaries to do what we dream of.

BYPASSING PEACHFORD

We were driving somewhere to have her repaired.
But, we weren't driving her. She was in the ambulance.
The pills were still in the top drawer of her nightstand.
My sister-in-law, the nurse, didn't even bother
to check her pulse—no other advice
than *call 911* when my brother said *overdose*.
But, I wasn't even in the car. It was my father
and brother. Mother was in the ambulance.
I was in Athens working for the week.
Father didn't call until the next day.
Mother, in the background insisting,
It didn't happen, not that way.

ODE TO LILITH

And the rib, which the Lord God had taken from man,
made he a woman, and brought her unto the man.

Genesis does not mention you.
You too were created of dust.
Folklore whispers that you wouldn't obey.
If mentioned, we might read
that you were banished from the garden,
not what really happened:
You wouldn't call Adam master,
lie beneath him. You asked
why he had to be on top,
and refused to be the first beggar
for the sake of a man's ego.
You reminded Adam that you
were made of the same dust,
created by the same God:
an equal beginning for equal partners.
Adam ran to his God.
You spoke the unspeakable name,
vanished, leaving Adam to slander:
Lilith, dark one who leads girls astray.
Lilith, temptress of new husbands.
Lilith, mother of all demons.
I toast to you.
Lilith, first to question.
Lilith, first protester.
Lilith, first to say,
I can leave. I can make my own way.

RULE #3 OF SEXUAL RELATIONS

Having sexual relations with a male animal is taboo
and punishable by death.
Does this apply if a man is dressed like an animal?
Seriously. I'm asking.
I'm bothered with this alleged fact. Well, not the taboo
part.
Taboo can be played like a game, but death is serious.
Death is permanent. So . . . does it count? I need to
know.
Halloween 2001. A party. Mark was a makeshift horse.
I was a cowboy.
All night I smacked his ass, said, *Giddy up, or*
I'll give you some spur.
After a few drinks it was, *Mark's hung like a horse.*
Everyone laughed, but some asked, *Really?*
I left with, *That's why this cowboy walks bowlegged.*

ADDENDS

Kim claims she woke him from the dead.
I tell her this guy isn't Lazarus.
She isn't Jesus.
He's a man in an unhappy marriage.
She's a woman in an unhappy marriage.
I don't need to be a math major
to work this equation.
The sum is not salvation.

FURIOUS CLEANING

after Maureen Seaton's "Furious Cooking"

It's the kind of cleaning that begins
with spitting, yelling, and cursing

because you can't believe he—
you—let it get so damn bad.

You inventory the papers, clothes, random
plates, and the lilies he bought to make you smile—

label everything *his* or *mine.*
His is destined for the garbage

bag you open with a fast swoop.
Air doesn't even fill the bag

before you sling the first item inside
looking for the next version of him

while eyeing those fucking lilies.
It's the kind of cleaning

that makes you sweat like working in the yard,
makes you stop to catch your breath.

The kind that is cathartic like a Sexton poem,
serves retribution like a Dante punishment,

cleanses like bleach on the floor.
I remember my mother standing at the sink

staring into her task of diluting bleach,
then on hands and knees scrubbing

an already spotless floor.
Tears fell from her eyes

as she dipped sponge in water,
mumbled *the bathroom is next*

all while cursing my father's name,
cleaning every spot named Christina.

LOSING AT CARDS

I wasn't out to hurt—I was out to destroy—
trust, friendships—spread misery like fertilizer
when I recited to my ex-boyfriend the inscription
he wrote in a card to his best friend—
proof I fucked my ex's best friend.

I confessed this to my grandmother
as we played Rummy.
Be careful not to set fire to a friend's house,
she warned as she drew from the deck.
He's not a friend, I replied.
You loved him once.
He'll always be a friend of your heart.
I studied my hand—kept to silence.
Honey, it isn't wise to start a fire
when your own house is just down the street.

THE LIST

I want a man
who'll sweep me off my feet on day one
but wait weeks before easing
me onto my back.
I want a man
who'll know monogamy isn't a type of wood,
who'll smile when he sees me approach
and meet me in the rain for a kiss.
I want a man
who'll like my friends for their personalities
instead of liking them for me,
who'll surprise me at work with lunch
before I surprise him.
I want a man
who'll take me home to meet his parents,
tell me his mother and sisters
will love me, and for once a man
will actually be right,
a man who'll grin when he hears me singing
Dolly's "Here You Come Again" and sing
along for a line or two,
who's graduated high school, attended college,
and still has a desire to learn,
a man who'll give his brutal opinion on my poems
instead of blowing smoke up my ass,
after all, that's what friends are for.
I want a man
who'll make love to me three times a week
and fuck me a minimum of four,
remember Anne Sexton is my favorite poet,
accept that I don't eat grits or gravy,

and realize the obsessive sensitivity I have regarding
my weight and not comment on the topic
in English or any other language.
I want a man
who wants two children and would
rather have his dick caught in a blender
than name them after a season,
who'll understand I love to talk, live to talk,
talk a lot, but listen just as well.
I want a man
who'll take me dancing and never
take his eyes off me.

FAGGOT

I own the word
like you own your name,
let it roll off my tongue
and grate you like cheese.
Faggot.
I said it.
You heard me.
It's the word you want
to use against me,
pour over my body
like boiling water.
Baby, I can handle the heat.
The word I once used
against my cousins:
Anthony. Faggot.
Brian. Faggot.
Lamar. Faggot.
It even tried to haunt:
Dustin. Faggot.
But I,
I deal the word
like a shark in Vegas.

I SHOULD WRITE SOAP OPERAS

My neighbor, well technically she isn't my neighbor
since she lives on the other side of the building, two
    floors below,
appeared with a baby a few weeks ago.
I've been meaning to tell Paul about the baby,
but the daily hum drum of life—work, rest, write—
has blocked my thoughts, but today,
we were walking Daisy and turned a corner
and there she was—baby strapped to chest
with its legs swinging. I think it might be a boy,
but I'm not sure. All the other times I've seen it,
it's been covered in a red blanket, which is no help
since red is like yellow where babies are concerned.
Anyway, I'm losing track of my point.
I think the baby is stolen.
Paul tells me she is probably babysitting.
I say, *She probably stole it.* Then add,
But not from another country,
as if this legitimizes my comment.
Paul rolls his eyes and tells me she can steal
the baby in one of my poems, but this is not
why I am writing this poem. I'll admit
I'm the kind of guy who enjoys a giggle
when I hear about someone objecting at a wedding.
I'll admit I've watched soap operas since I was eight
and rooted for the villain most of the time.
I adored Vivian and Sami on *Days of Our Lives.*
My mother threatened to quit taping episodes
when I cheered for them. You might not know,
Sami stole her baby sister. Well, she stole her half baby
    sister,

but only she and her cheating mother Marlena
knew about the half part. I'm not saying this is the case
with the mystery baby in my building. I'm only
saying it's OK not to accept what's in front of you
      at face value.

MEETING JUDY BLUME

With *Are you there God? It's me, Margaret.*
in hand, I waited patiently in line.
Judy had a volunteer pass us note cards.
We wrote the personalized messages
we wanted inscribed in our books.
Judy looked at my card—a puzzled look
came across her face, as if she had passed
a puppies for sale sign
when there were kittens in the basket.
I explained, *It's a gift.*
I thought it'd be fun.
Still appearing baffled,
with pursed lip, she said,
You realize this is a children's book.
I fumbled, *Ms. Blume, we, the gays,*
love you. She wrote the message,
handed me the book and said,
I love most of you too.

NOTES

The first line of "Bypassing Peachford" is from Denise Duhamel's "David Lemieux."

The epigraph of "Ode to Lilith" is from Genesis 2:22.

The first line of "Rule #3 Of Sexual Relations" is from Denise Duhamel's "Lawless Pantoum."

The eighth line of "Losing at Cards" is from Kenneth Koch's "Some General Instructions."

ACKNOWLEDGMENTS

Many thanks to the following literary journals and anthologies in which some of these poems, at times in earlier incarnations, appeared:

Assaracus: "Bad Fruit," "Bypassing Peachford," and "This Poem Wants To Be Censored"

Divining Divas: 100 Gay Men on Their Muses: "Ode to Lilith"

The Impossible Archetype: "On Line Dancing Night At The Gay Bar I Think Of My Grandma"

Mollyhouse: "Furious Cleaning"

OCHO: "Meeting Judy Blume"

Ouroboros: "Memo," "The List," and "Wanting To Come Out"

Qarrtsiluni: "Faggot" and "I Should Write Soap Operas"

The Queer South: LGBTQ Writers on the American South: "Signs"

Redheaded Stepchild: "Addends"

South Florida Poetry Journal: "To Teri Hatcher With Love"

Subtle Tea: "Signs"

Whiskey Island: "Rule #3 Of Sexual Relations"

Heartfelt gratitude to the Harbor Editions team and Allison Blevins for their dedication to poetry and giving this chapbook a home.

BF Chris, thank you for always saying yes when I say, *I've written a new poem. Want to hear it?* Your support means more than you'll ever know.

Beth, I will never be able to extend the appropriate level of gratitude to you. Thank you for your friendship, unwavering support, and feedback on many of my poems.

BFF Chris, for someone who isn't a poet, you have a poet's mind for feedback. Thank you for being you and our soon-to-be twenty years of friendship.

Julie, thank you for giving this chapbook a little TLC.

Dustin Brookshire, a finalist for the 2021 Scotti Merrill Award, is the founder/editor of *Limp Wrist* and curator of the Wild & Precious Life Series, a Zoom-based poetry reading series. He is the author of the chapbooks *Love Most Of You Too* (Harbor Editions, 2021) and *To The One Who Raped Me* (Sibling Rivalry Press, 2012). Dustin's work has been nominated for a Pushcart Prize and been published in *Assaracus*, *Whiskey Island*, *Mollyhouse*, *The West Review*, *Oddball*, *Gulf Stream Magazine*, *Redheaded Stepchild*, *SubtleTea*, *Ocho*, *Oranges & Sardines*, *Ouroboros*, *Qarrtsiluni*, *Blue Fifth Review*, and other publications. He has been anthologized in *Divining Divas: 100 Gay Men on their Muses* (Lethe Press, 2012) and *The Queer South: LGBTQ Writes on the American South* (Sibling Rivalry Press, 2014). Visit him online at dustinbrookshire.com.

Made in the USA
Columbia, SC
31 July 2024

39770225R00024